Bygone PERTH

Guthrie Hutton

Pictures of painters and decorators, like this one by a Perth photographer, are rare. The seated man is trimming a roll of wallpaper, a tedious and easily botched task made necessary because early papers were printed with margins which had to be cut off before hanging.

© Guthrie Hutton 2005
First published in the United Kingdom, 2005,
by Stenlake Publishing Ltd.
Telephone: 01290 551122
Printed by Cordfall Ltd., Glasgow, G21 2QA

ISBN 1 84033 352 9

**The publishers regret that they cannot supply
copies of any pictures featured in this book.**

ACKNOWLEDGEMENTS

This is a follow-up volume to a smaller book, *Old Perth*, which I compiled in 1995, and I have again enjoyed tramping the streets of the Fair City in pursuit of further information from its past. I have enjoyed, too, revisiting the A. K. Bell Library. It is a splendid resource with unfailingly helpful and friendly staff who I must thank for digging out material for me, often one item following another in rapid succession. I must also thank Alan Brotchie for assisting with pictures.

FURTHER READING

Aitken, John, *Above the Tay Bridges*, 1986
Blower, Alan, *British Railway Tunnels*, 1964
Brodie, Ian, *Steamers of the Tay*, 2003
Brotchie, Alan W., *Tramways of the Tay Valley*, 1965
Brotchie, Alan W., *Wheels Around Perth*, 2001
Findlay, W. H., *Heritage of Perth*, 1996
Fothergill, Rhoda, *The Inches of Perth*
Graham-Campbell, David, *Perth, The Fair City*, 1994
Haynes, Nick, *Perth & Kinross, An Architectural Guide*, 2000
Munro, Denis, *A Vision of Perth*, 2000
Perthshire Advertiser, *Know Your Perth, Volumes 1 & 2*
Simpson, W. Douglas, *A History of Saint John's Kirk, Perth*, 1958
Stavert, Marion L., *Perth, A Short History*, 1991
Vallance, H. A., *The Highland Railway*, 1963
Watson, Norman, *Perth in Old Picture Postcards*, 1993

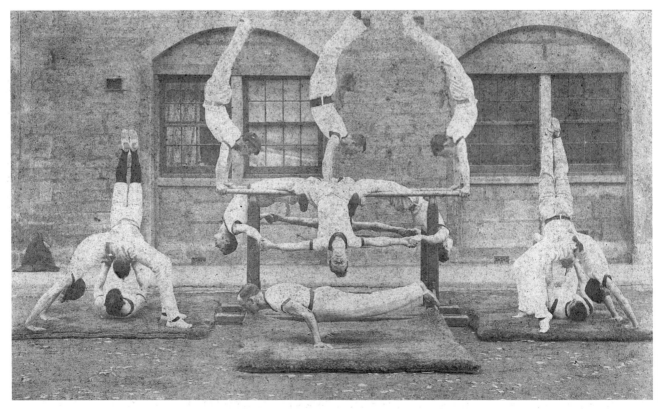

Early twentieth century Perth gymnasts display their prowess.

INTRODUCTION

Perth developed at the highest point on the River Tay that ships could navigate to, and the lowest point on the broad estuary where a bridge could be built. Not that the latter task was easy, with a number of early structures being swept away before one could be built of sufficient strength to defy the river. That bridge was at the leading edge of technology in its day, but as techniques and materials improved engineers gained the knowledge and skills to bridge the river at Dundee. They made a hash of it the first time around, but the success of the second railway bridge not only ended Perth's status as the lowest crossing point on the Tay, but also limited the height of sailing ships that could pass beneath. Perth could have stagnated, but instead it grew and has since added two new road bridges, Queen's and Friarton, to Dundee's one. With motor ships requiring less air draught than sailing vessels it is also thriving again as a port.

The original river crossing and harbour was guarded by a castle which was swept away in the early thirteenth century by one of the Tay's many floods. It was never rebuilt and instead the town sheltered behind stout walls. These in turn were surrounded by an artificial waterway, a lade taken from the River Almond which flowed toward the town before being divided, with one branch heading for the Tay down the northern side of the wall and the other flowing along its western and southern flanks. Thus confined by water and walls, the town grew until it filled every inch of ground that its spiritual protectors, the church, didn't occupy. A number of monasteries and nunneries were established both inside and outside the city walls, while St John's Church dominated the town centre. It was here, in 1559, that John Knox delivered a sermon that so aroused resentment of the overbearing church presence that it started a riot. The people stripped the church of its riches and smashed the images denounced as idolatrous by Knox, before going on to storm other church properties, looting them and gorging on the plentiful food they contained. It was the first act of the Reformation that transformed Scotland, and it happened in Perth.

For the next 200 years religiously motivated armies came and went from the city. Montrose passed by, but Cromwell's troops stayed and built a citadel on the South Inch, demolishing buildings, stripping the Inches of turf and removing the town cross to do so. The Jacobites headed south through Perth in 1715 and came back again pursued by Government troops. They returned in 1745 when Bonnie Prince Charlie stood by the rebuilt cross to declare his father as King James VIII before marching to Derby and back to defeat at Culloden.

The latter half of the eighteenth century was more peaceful, and Perth transformed itself by building the new bridge, razing the town walls and developing new streets, with elegant Georgian architecture offering a contrast to the earlier Scots vernacular. Perth's medieval lade became its primary source of industrial power in the nineteenth century, when dye works were set up beside it. Railways broke through the hills to cash in on Perth's strategic position and provide the town with a major industry in itself. The railway also encouraged other activities such as livestock sales and whisky production, and by developing banking and insurance services Perth found a way of making money out of money too.

So if the town felt threatened by Dundee's bridges (and it did), it coped as serenely with that threat as it had done with others before it, and no doubt will with the challenges of the future.

Today's vast increase in waste requires much larger refuse disposal vehicles than this post-Second World War double-cab street cleaning wagon, a state-of-the-art model at the time.

Few early buildings survived Scotland's turbulent past intact, and fewer still have remained in continuous use from the day they were built, but St John's Kirk in the middle of Perth is one. A church, thought to date from the early twelfth century, predated the present building, which was begun c.1440 and completed by the end of the century when the north porch, also known as the Halkerston Tower, was finished. At 200 feet long, 155 feet high and occupying the only open space in a congested warren of humble dwellings, it must have looked awesome. The contrast with the living conditions endured by the good folk of Perth must have contributed to the combustible effect that the spark ignited by Knox in 1559 had. Once they had exorcised their grievances, however, the people just got on with their lives and St John's Kirk settled down as a place of Protestant worship. The congested little city was split into three parishes and the church was divided by internal walls into three separate places of worship: East, West and Middle St John. In the 1920s one of Scotland's leading architects, Sir Robert Lorimer, led a substantial restoration programme which reunited the interior. It also incorporated a shrine of remembrance for Perthshire people who lost their lives during the First World War. Further renovations have been carried out since and the surrounding area pedestrianised so that only a few authorised cars are now allowed to park against the church walls.

To the east of St John's Kirk was a semi-enclosed area known as Market Square where an old city hall stood for just over 70 years before Perth Town Council decided to build a new one. The foundation stone was laid in June 1909 and the building was completed in 1911. This postcard, showing the 2,100-seat interior, was published to celebrate its opening in April of that year.

Prior to construction of the new city hall, a clutter of old buildings and closes was cleared away to create a new thoroughfare between High Street and South Street, named King Edward Street after the new king. His reign was short – 1901 to 1910 – and his death was marked by a memorial garden opposite the hall which had as its centrepiece a new mercat cross, designed to replicate that of Edinburgh. This was erected in 1913 and is still there, but the garden has gone and the St John's Centre now occupies the ground to the left of this early 1950s picture. Ironically, the pedestrianisation of King Edward Street had the effect of creating space for markets that was lost when the new hall was built on Market Square.

St John's Middle Church School in Meal Vennel was taken over by Perth School Board after the 1872 Education Act and became the Central District School. Hemmed in on all sides, the building was declared unsuitable by the Scottish Education Department in the 1890s. The school board looked at various options, eventually buying up some old tenement property adjacent to the school and clearing the site for a new three-storey building (illustrated here). This was opened in September 1901. All of the classrooms faced the same way to get the best light, the three on the ground floor each accommodating 72 infants, while those on the upper floors provided room for 60 pupils. The paired desks were set on raised staging so that there was no hiding place for shirkers and cheats at the back of the room.

Perth's street layout has changed significantly from the tightly packed wynds, closes and vennels of the medieval town, but High Street has always been the principal thoroughfare. It ran from the city wall in the west to the river in the east at the point where the early bridges and harbour were. At the river end, the old tolbooth sat across the end of the street with arched pends underneath for through passage. Although that structure has gone and there has been much building and rebuilding over the years, the street's slightly kinked line remains, which helps to convey a sense of its past. It is seen here looking west with Wood's shop and restaurant at the extreme right, on the corner of George Street.

John Wood established his bakers and confectioners business in 1845 with a bakehouse in Skinnergate, but that was soon outgrown and he moved to Watergate. Similarly, the shop on the corner of High Street and George Street began in a small way, but expansion was made necessary by the high demand for Wood's cakes, especially the wine biscuits, and the addition of a restaurant. Although Wood's is no longer there, the attractive first floor window remains.

George Street cut a swathe through part of the old city when it was laid out in the 1770s to provide a link between the new bridge and High Street. It became the location of some of Perth's most important buildings: the first post office; the prestigious Royal George Hotel; the art gallery and museum; and the headquarters of the Perth Banking Company, which were graced by this imposing frontage. The building was erected c.1857, a date which coincides with the company becoming part of the Union Bank, an amalgam of a number of smaller banking companies from across Scotland.

Paterson's music shop was next door to the bank. The company was established in Edinburgh in the 1830s and became one of Scotland's foremost music stores, with branches in all the major towns and cities. Paterson's first shop in Perth was opened in the late 1850s, but this soon proved too small, prompting a move to a new site in Princes Street. This shop had a handsomely decorated frontage, but the interior was deliberately restrained to show off the fine pianos and other instruments to best effect. The company clearly believed in attractive shopfronts, moving to this site in George Street with its impressive windows c.1907. The window on the left-hand side of the picture is still there.

PATERSON, SONS & CO., THE LEADING SCOTTISH MUSIC DEALERS,
New Premises at 26, George Street, **PERTH.**
And at DUNDEE, EDINBURGH, GLASGOW, ARBROATH, ABERDEEN Etc.

When King Edward VII died in 1910 and his successor, George V, was announced, a ceremony took place at the Cross (the site of the old mercat cross in High Street at its junction with Kirkgate and Skinnergate). Perth's cross had been destroyed by Cromwell's troops in 1651, and its replacement was removed in 1765 to clear the way for traffic, so the dignitaries had to make do with the middle of the street (and stop the traffic altogether!). They walked in procession from the county buildings in Tay Street, up South Street, along Scott Street and down High Street to the Cross, where Lord Provost Macnab read the proclamation. The sunny day no doubt helped to swell the crowds.

This ceremony to lay the foundation stone for the rebuilding of the Guild Hall in High Street took place in 1907. The Merchant Guild, later known as the Guildry Incorporation of Perth, had its origins in the royal charter granted to Perth by King William the Lion *c.*1210. The guild effectively formed the first local authority and continued to exercise influence in civic administration until the Burgh Reform Act of 1833. After that the Dean of Guild Court acted as the buildings authority and administered common law regarding property disputes until local government reorganisation in 1975.

Ceremonies to announce new monarchs or lay foundation stones attracted large crowds, as did parades and processions, which were familiar sights in High Street at least up until the First World War. Here a wartime recruiting march makes its way across the junction with Scott and Kinnoull Streets.

Opposite: Before Friarton Bridge was opened in 1978 to carry traffic going to and from the north-east past the city, all cross-river traffic was funnelled through the centre of Perth, making life uncomfortable for pedestrians such as this woman scurrying across High Street in front of a lorry. Shopping is now a more relaxed activity in the pedestrianised street. In the 1970s Marks & Spencer's moved across High Street to a new location just to the right of the lorry. Prior to the new store being built, archaeologists were given time to investigate the site, and many interesting finds were unearthed, giving an insight into life in the medieval city. This knowledge has been added to by subsequent excavations at a number of development sites around the old city.

The Grand Hotel on the corner of High Street and Kinnoull Street promoted itself as the 'most central in the city' – a description somewhat dependant on where people thought the centre was. It was a temperance hotel with a restaurant geared to providing 'commercial dinners' as well as meals for customers in less of a hurry. Its horse bus met all trains and 'boots' was on hand to carry passengers' luggage. Cyclists were provided with 'every comfort'.

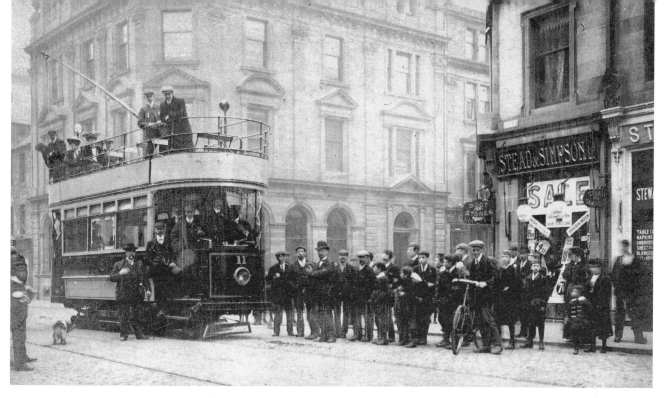

Horse-drawn tram services commenced in Perth in 1895 and the system was electrified in 1905. The absence of a destination board on this tram at the junction of High Street with Scott and Kinnoull Streets suggests that the picture was taken just before the electric trams started to operate, possibly on an inspection run. There were two principal routes: one ran between Scone and Cherrybank going through the city centre along George, High and South Methven Streets. The other went from a terminus at the Cross, at the east end of High Street, along South Methven and King Streets to Craigie. At the time of electrification the tracks were also taken along North Methven Street to Dunkeld Road.

The trams ceased to operate in 1929 and their nemesis, a bus, is seen here at the Scott and Kinnoull Street junction with High Street (looking east). The Grand Hotel, which occupied the building on the left, stopped trading in the early 1920s and Stead & Simpson's shoe shop on the ground floor became a fruit and flower shop in the early 1930s. On the right is the former post office building, erected in 1898 to replace an earlier post office at No. 2 High Street, which had itself opened in 1862, taking over from the original post office in George Street. The post office moved again in 1973 to new premises in South Street.

A couple of horse-drawn trams can be seen in the distance on the right of this 1901 view of High Street looking east from its junction with South Methven Street.

Looking west from High Street's junction with Scott and Kinnoull Streets, the distinctive spire of St Paul's Church stands out as a focal point. It remains a special element of Perth's townscape, but is now in need of some loving care and attention. The church was built in 1806/7 on a site adjacent to the old lade. At one time the lade was widened and deepened from the river up to this point and some old mooring rings were found well below street-level here, suggesting the former existence of a landing stage. There was also a gate in the old city walls here known as the Turret Brig Port, a name that suggests some kind of drawbridge over the lade, but it disappeared when the walls were demolished in the 1760s.

Robert Henderson was a game dealer, poulterer, fishmonger and fruit and potato merchant. He even provided 'fresh Norwegian ice', a dangerous trade for the men who brought these unstable cargoes across the North Sea. Closer to hand were Henderson's nurseries at Hillyland and the gentlemen's estates which supplied the quantities of game and rabbits. Henderson's shop was on the corner of High Street and South Methven Street. The building, erected in 1903, still bears Henderson's RH monogram.

Old High Street is seen here looking east from its junction with Caledonian and St Catherine's Roads. On the right is Alexander McCowan's drapery and further down the street is a low building which was, and still is, the premises of iron and steel merchants W. & D. Peddie. St Paul's Church can be seen in the distance.

One part of Perth that has changed radically in recent years is the area of industrial works and railway yards to the west of the city centre. The changes are such that if this funeral was taking place today the mourners would be entering a supermarket car park and filling station forecourt. They were presumably in procession from one of the city churches to Wellshill Cemetery and are seen here early in the twentieth century at the west end of Old High Street.

Automotive engineers Ferguson & Batchelor, whose name can be seen in the background of this picture of St Catherine's Road, took over the premises of the Perth Preserve Works in 1930, which gives some clue to the date of the picture. The street name came from a former chapel in the vicinity, while the tenement in the left foreground, Moir's Buildings, was named after its builder, James Moir. His son, Alexander, ran a licensed grocery in the corner shop and the shop next door was a dairy run by Mrs Alexandra Mitchell. The shops had changed owners and functions by the time the buildings were demolished and the site redeveloped in the early 1990s.

The run of buildings on the left-hand side of the picture of St Catherine's Road is seen from the rear on the left of this picture of a funeral procession in Old High Street. It is alas not known who is being honoured in either this ceremony or the one on the previous page. They are large affairs, so it is likely that the deceased on both occasions was someone of stature. Funeral processions like these, where mourners follow the hearse at a slow walk, are rare today, having been largely superseded by cremations.

The Salutation Hotel in South Street, seen here between its darker coloured neighbours, prides itself on being the 'Oldest Established Hotel in Scotland', having opened its doors in 1699. To support the claim it has a fireplace dating from that time, but the rest of the structure is not so old. It is formed of two halves: that nearest the camera dates from the eighteenth century and was remodelled in the nineteenth, while the other half, with the splendid arched window, largely dates from *c.*1800. Two kilted Highlanders in first floor niches point to the hotel's Jacobite links. Bonnie Prince Charlie is reputed to have stayed there and a meeting between the Prince and a Colonel Bower at the Salutation was given in evidence against the colonel when he was tried for supporting the Jacobites.

'The Salvation Army Songster Brigade, Perth'. Early critics dismissed the Salvation Army as 'brass band Christianity', but the mix of uplifting music and down-to-earth missionary work amongst society's poor made them a force to be reckoned with. Such was their support in November 1904 that the *Perthshire Advertiser* was able to report that 'an immense crowd' had gathered at the corner of South and King Edward Streets to witness the memorial stone being laid for the new citadel. The building gave these songsters and other activists a place from which to operate, and the Salvation Army still has a presence on the site.

As its former name, South High Street, implies, South Street was a principal thoroughfare through the medieval city, making Perth unusual – if not unique in Scotland – in having what amounted to two high streets. It is seen here looking west toward the site of the gate in the city wall known as either the West Port or South Street Port, at the intersection with King and South Methven Streets and County Place. The picture can be dated to sometime after 1922/23 when boot and shoemaker Henry P. Tyler moved his shop from High Street to South Street. The oval inset shows South Street looking west at its junction with Scott Street.

The Coronation of King George V in 1911 gave the people of Perth an excuse to dress up and have a party, and they decorated the city too. Bands and floats representing various aspects of local and national life formed a parade which is seen here passing through a representation of the old South Street Port.

Perth Carriage Works in Canal Street, and latterly also Princes Street, was established in 1797. It came under the ownership of William Thomson c.1854, and he built its reputation for workmanship and style, placing great stress on the seasoning of wood and allowing the large stock of assorted timbers to mature for at least three years before use. The most celebrated product designed and built at the works was the 'Perth' four-wheeled dogcart, which with the addition of a hood was ideal for use in India or the colonies. The company also made broughams, landaus, wagonettes and other vehicles, including this splendid van for the City of Perth Co-operative Society.

William Robertson, engineers, whose principal trade appears to have been in agricultural machinery, moved into the former Canal Street premises of the Perth Carriage Works c.1910, although it is not known when or for what occasion the workforce decorated this traction engine. Canal Street takes its name from the old town lade which ran alongside the city wall. This southern arm of the lade was widened and deepened as a navigable canal, allowing boats from the Tay to reach the works and warehouses here. The street replaced the lade in the 1790s.

Whisky is one of Perth's major industries, but in July 1919 it was in the news for all the wrong reasons when Arthur Bell & Son's bond in Canal Street went up in flames. Houses in the adjacent Horner's Lane were destroyed and only about twelve barrels of whisky were saved from the gutted bond. At the height of the blaze, rivers of flaming whisky ran into the street and on one occasion engulfed machinery which had been removed from a warehouse in case that caught alight. A bus, dustcarts and Love's furniture vans were all pressed into service to bring sand from nearby builders' yards to form dams to contain the burning spirit. After the fire the street looked like a beach and so children, being children, made sandcastles!

Initially a plumbing and electrical business based in Mill Street, Frew & Co. started selling Ford cars in 1910 and became established in Canal Street/Princes Street after the First World War. Most vehicles did well, but tractor sales were slow until the Second World War prompted changes in farming practices. Farmers needing machinery for a particular task could obtain it from Frew's who operated a fleet of tractors and equipment for the Department of Agriculture. After the war tractor sales and servicing increased, as did other branches of the business, which necessitated a move from these cramped Canal Street premises to Riggs Road in 1958 and, in 1990, to United Auctions' former site. The company was sold to Macrae & Dick ten years later.

Princes Street was created c.1770 to provide a route through the city from the new Perth Bridge to the Edinburgh Road. In this view from c.1925, Victoria Street is seen just beyond the car on the left with the Victoria Hotel – 'no more popular hotel than the Vic' – on the corner. The spire of St John the Baptist Episcopal Church can be seen poking above the roofs on the right.

The Episcopal Church has had a presence in Princes Street since 1796 when a chapel was built there. This soon became too small to accommodate the number of worshippers and so, in 1851, St John the Baptist Church was erected to the designs of the brothers Hay, architects from Liverpool.

The B. B. Cinerama, otherwise known as the Victoria Picture Palace, opened in Victoria Street in August 1910. It was closed spectacularly in January 1922 by a fire thought to have been caused by a dropped cigarette end. Little remained of the building after the blaze, but most of the valuable films were saved and the projection room survived largely intact behind fire protection measures – presumably designed to safeguard the auditorium if the projector had gone up in flames. The building was originally a Free Church, but its congregation moved out in the 1880s to the new St Leonard's in the Fields Church in Marshall Place. After that it had been used as an auction room and a roller skating rink.

The building in Watergate known as Kinnoull Lodging or the Dower House must be the one of the most photographed old houses in Perth. Such exposure suggests that its value was, if not fully understood, at least partly appreciated. It was a classic old Scots townhouse with a timber frontage to the upper storeys, supported by timber posts from the street. It dated from the early 1600s and was the last such house in Perth until its demolition in the 1960s – a decade when the Scots destroyed more of their own heritage than any invading army ever did!

Trams to and from Craigie were clearly not so frequent as to deter a boy from parking his bicycle across the tracks in this picture of King Street, *c*.1912. Perhaps he got the bike from Harry Christie's Cycle Works on the right, which if Mr Christie's publicity was to be believed was the best place to buy or sell a cycle. His shop was on the corner of Charterhouse Lane, a name derived from the Carthusian monastery that stood here before the Reformation, marked by a memorial across the road at the King James VI Hospital. It is hidden by the trees on the left, as is St Leonard's Church which was built in 1834 and is now an auction room.

The West or South Street Port, which gave access through the city walls, was situated where South Street becomes County Place, while King and South Methven Streets, which also meet here, perpetuate the line of the demolished walls. The large corner block with the Central Bar on the ground floor was built *c*.1900 to the designs of Edinburgh architects McLaren & MacKay. The tobacconist and fancy goods shop next door was one of a number run by Mrs Ann Harris.

South Methven Street was a busy shopping street prior to the First World War when this picture was taken – and even during the war when the two advertisements below appeared. Young & Campbell occupied a shop on the east side of the street in the building seen to the left of the central lamp post and sign. The Perthshire Rubber Co. was across the street in a large classical warehouse building erected *c.*1840. It was later used by seedsmen Alexander & Brown whose business was established in the late nineteenth century in High Street, moved to Scott Street, back to High Street and then to South Methven Street.

Having rounded the corner from High Street, a Cherrybank-bound tram heads along South Methven Street with the domed Royal Bank building beyond. St Paul's Church can be seen creeping in on the left and the Bee Restaurant is on the right. Now the Bee Bar, it used to offer breakfasts, lunches and teas 'at any time' in its enlarged and redecorated dining room, which it claimed to be the 'finest in the city'.

Sharp's Institution was named after John Sharp of Barnhill who left money from his estate in a trust deed which was used to set up a school. This opened in 1860 and was run by trustees who maintained its independent status after the Education Act of 1872 set up school boards to oversee the provision of universal education. In 1910 the trustees agreed to abandon the school's independence and bring it under the umbrella of Perth School Board. At the time the roll stood at 245 junior and 175 senior pupils, studying a full range of academic and craft subjects. The year that this display of pupils' work was presented was thus the last that Sharp's was an independent institution. It became part of Perth Academy in 1915.

When legislation was introduced making local authorities responsible for providing public libraries, Perth Town Council was short of cash. Their difficulties were solved when Professor Archibald Sandeman, an academic and member of the prominent Sandeman family, left a bequest in excess of £30,000. The Sandeman Library, as it was known, was opened by Lord Rosebery in Kinnoull Street in 1898 and continued to serve the city until 1994, when the A. K. Bell Library in York Place was opened. The North Church can be seen half-hidden to the right of the library in Mill Street.

The North Church in the upper picture was built by a United Presbyterian congregation in 1880 to replace their old church, seen here, which had been erected in 1792 to hold 1,400 worshipers. It in turn replaced the congregation's original church, built in 1749. United Presbyterians belonged to the Secession Church which came into being when its leaders broke away from the Church of Scotland at a

ceremony at Gairney Bridge, near Kinross, in 1733. Perth's North Church was set up following a split within the Secession Church itself, but this was healed in 1847 when the United Presbyterian Church was formed. Prior to that, in 1843, the Established Church was split again when the Free Church broke away, but the factions began to reunite during the twentieth century and the North Church eventually became part of the Church of Scotland.

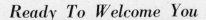

Ready To Welcome You

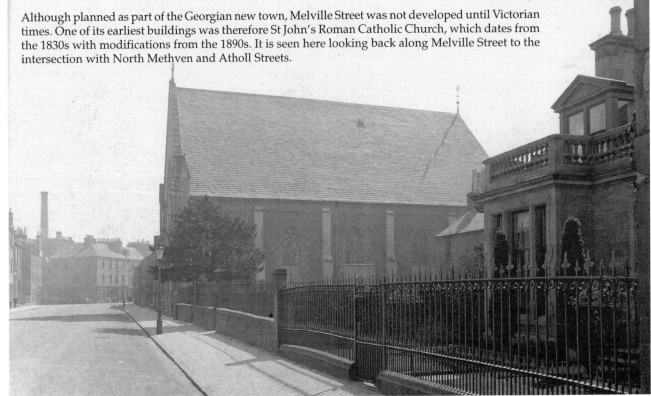

The New Lunch and Tearoom at Atholl Street Corner . . .

When the main business of your day is over and the time comes to relax, make **ADIE'S** your rendezvous for **AFTERNOON** or **HIGH TEA**. A Varied Menu appetisingly served. **MORNING TEAS.   LUNCHES.**

Wm. Adie & Sons,
BAKERS and CONFECTIONERS
SERVICE UNTIL 5.30 P.M. EVERY WEEK-DAY. INCLUDING SATURDAYS AND WEDNESDAYS.

Vienna bread, baked in a special electrically heated oven, was a speciality of William Adie's bakery in the 1930s when this advertisement exhorted people to patronise the firm's tea room on the corner of Atholl and Melville Streets.

Following completion of the new bridge in 1771, Perth burst out of its medieval confines with the building of several new streets like North Methven Street. It ran from Murray Street to Atholl Street, which formed a broad approach to the bridge. The needs of modern traffic have further transformed these originally elegant thoroughfares into busy roads which are never quiet and forever on the move.

Although planned as part of the Georgian new town, Melville Street was not developed until Victorian times. One of its earliest buildings was therefore St John's Roman Catholic Church, which dates from the 1830s with modifications from the 1890s. It is seen here looking back along Melville Street to the intersection with North Methven and Atholl Streets.

Tucked in behind the busy main streets and elegant new town were some old lanes, rows and vennels where poorer people continued to live into the age when cameras were available to record them. To modern eyes the buildings look to be full of character, although doubtless they were often little better than slums. The location of the top right picture is not known; top left is Thummle Row; lower left is Cherry Lane; and lower right is the house in Mill Wynd made famous by Sir Walter Scott who chose it as Hal o' the Wynd's house for the *Fair Maid of Perth*.

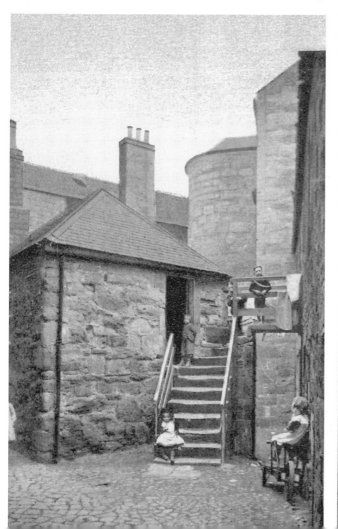

FENWICK'S LUNCHEON & TEA-ROOMS.
9, COUNTY PLACE & TEA ROOM AT 27 ST JOHN STREET.
PERTH.

THE ROSE ROOM

APPROACH TO TEA ROOM

The road leading west from South Street changes name three times in a short distance from County Place to York Place and then Glasgow Road. The oval view shows County Place looking west from South Street with, in the distance, a large domed tenement building which was erected in 1907 on the corner of York Place and New Row. The south-facing County Place shops have had to protect their windows from the midday sun by drawing out their awnings. One of these, at the end of the run of two-storey buildings in the centre of the picture, was A. Fenwick & Sons bakery, tea room and restaurant.

The Tay Iron Works of Market Street and New Row was established by George Barker in the 1870s. It was mainly concerned with supplying and servicing the agricultural industry, employing a range of skilled workers including machine makers, engineers and millwrights. They produced a variety of equipment including manure distributors, turnip drills, spring-tooth harrows and implements like the rollers seen in the drawing. The works' best-selling product appears to have been the thistle and bracken cutter. Farmers regarded thistles as a pest and they liked the Tay Iron Works' machine because its rotating blades turned in the same direction of travel as the machine and could thus pick up and chop broken and downtrodden thistles as well as those standing tall. The works also acted as an agent for other manufacturers, supplying threshing mills, barn machinery, cultivators and swathe turners. It strove to keep up with the latest developments through the early years of the twentieth century by marketing oil-driven engines, suction gas plants, and pumps like the one seen here.

LAND ROLLERS
With CAST-METAL CYLINDERS.

Supplied with Wood or Tubular Iron Shafts

Constructed of Steel Frame, & Axle and
CAST-IRON ENDS and ROLLER CYLINDERS

SIZES & PRICES :-

ROLLER,	6 ft wide by 18 in. diameter	£7.0.0
Do.	7 ft ,, 18 in. ,,	7.16.6
Do.	6 ft ,, 20 in. ,,	7.12.6
Do.	6½ ,, 21 in. ,,	8.0.0
Do.	7½ ,, 21 in. ,,	9.2.6

STRONG TWO-HORSE ROLLERS
with 2 barrels and low Down Frames

GEORGE BARKER   Tay Iron Works PERTH.   TO ORDER.

The County & City Hospital building has had a chequered history. Built to the designs of city architect William McKenzie, the foundation stone was laid in August 1836 and the first patients were admitted just over two years later. 'Royal' was added to the title in 1888, but the building was soon struggling to cope with demand and was replaced by the new Perth Royal Infirmary in 1914. The outbreak of the First World War soon after, however, meant that the old building remained in use as a Red Cross or VAD (Voluntary Aid Detachment) hospital. The detachment met trains which arrived in Perth early in the morning, so that few people saw them, and took the 100 or more wounded servicemen on board to hospital by ambulance or car. The old hospital building was later taken over as the headquarters of Perth County Council, and in 1994 the facade and entrance hall were incorporated into the new A. K. Bell Library.

A parade of what appear to be postmen is seen marching past the former Trinity Church in York Place. The church was built in 1860 for a congregation of the United Presbyterian Church. After nearly 200 years of division and discord the Protestant churches reunited in the twentieth century, and this, coupled with dwindling congregations, saw many church buildings become empty and disused. Trinity Church nonetheless survived as a place of worship and is currently used by the Church of the Nazarene.

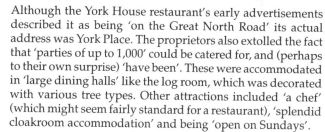

Although the York House restaurant's early advertisements described it as being 'on the Great North Road' its actual address was York Place. The proprietors also extolled the fact that 'parties of up to 1,000' could be catered for, and (perhaps to their own surprise) 'have been'. These were accommodated in 'large dining halls' like the log room, which was decorated with various tree types. Other attractions included 'a chef' (which might seem fairly standard for a restaurant), 'splendid cloakroom accommodation' and being 'open on Sundays'.

The Waverley Hotel, on the corner of York Place and Caledonian Road, was ideally placed to provide accommodation for farmers and dealers attending the nearby livestock sales. Its 22 bedrooms were 'large and airy', there was a ladies' drawing room, a smoking room and a 'spacious' dining room that acquired a reputation as the place to go for that mainstay of Scottish cuisine, the high tea. Concerns that the hotel might become a homeless hostel surfaced when it changed hands early in 2005.

Perth's reputation as a centre for livestock sales was enhanced by record prices reached for animals like Lord Lovat's red shorthorn bull Broadhooks Champion. It was sold by Macdonald, Fraser & Co. in February 1906 to a bidder from Buenos Aires who beat off other Argentinean and Irish competition to secure the animal for 1,500 guineas. Prices kept on rising until 60,000 guineas was paid for an Aberdeen Angus bull in 1963 (rumour has it that the beast was infertile!). Macdonald, Fraser & Co. began in Mill Street in 1858 and moved to a new market off Caledonian Road, beside the railway, in 1875. Now under new ownership and no longer reliant on railways for the movement of animals, the market has moved to a site near Huntingtower.

FECHNEY INDUSTRIAL SCHOOL BAND, PERTH.
"Constitutional" Office, Perth.

H. Wadsworth, Bandmaster
(late of H.M. Coldstream Guards' Band).

The Fechney Industrial School was opened in 1864. The aim of such schools was to help youngsters with a low aptitude for mainstream education by concentrating on practical skills. Industrial schools also taught band music and at the Fechney the standard of playing was regarded as very high. The band played at functions throughout the city and as this picture shows it was clearly a source of pride. The Fechney, which could accommodate 200–300 boys, closed in 1922.

Opposite: The decision to build a new Royal Infirmary was taken in 1909 when moves were instigated to secure an eleven-acre site at Tullylumb, which was still largely rural then as these pictures show. The buildings were designed by Glasgow architect James Millar and consisted of four two-storey ward blocks linked to an admission and outpatient department block by a 128-yard covered corridor. There was a three-storey administrative block with a directors' boardroom, apartments for the house surgeon and matron, rooms for key staff and a nurses' sick room. There was also a nurses' home, a kitchen block with staff dining hall and bedrooms, and a laundry with a disinfector which could handle items as large as a bed. Other buildings housed an isolation block, laboratory, stores, power station and mortuary. A block containing two large wards for children was added before construction was completed.

The infirmary was ceremonially opened on 10 July 1914 by King George V, who is seen here, centre, with Queen Mary and the Duke of Atholl (left, wearing the uniform), Lord Lieutenant of the county. The royal party arrived in Perth by train from Dundee and paraded through the streets before opening the infirmary. In County Place a suffragette from Glasgow ran out from the crowd and made for the royal car. The chauffeur (that could be him on the extreme right, seated behind the wheel of a car) swerved, while one of the escorting troopers of the Scottish Horse (that could be them on the left) penned her in while the police moved in to make an arrest. Within a few weeks those same troopers would be fighting a war of attrition against a more dangerous foe than a politically inspired young woman.

Cobbles, also known in Scotland as 'causeys' (causeway stones), being laid between tram tracks beside the Glasgow Road post office, which was on the corner of Rose Crescent. Alexander Dewar's bakery is on the left. Although it appears posed, the picture shows how men worked in an almost synchronous way with a hand tool which they used to lever and knock the heavy stones into position. The picture was taken at the time the tram system was electrified in 1905.

Rose Crescent, a street of mainly late nineteenth and early twentieth century semi-detached villas, is seen here looking toward Glasgow Road from the junction with Western Avenue. The Royal Infirmary is off to the right of the picture, which is thought to date from the 1920s.

Hamilton House, off Glasgow Road, was built in 1865 and after a succession of owners became a youth hostel. It was up for sale again in 2005.

PERTH YOUTH HOSTEL   381

Will write you soon

Manse of Middle St. John, Perth.

Bazaar, 14, 15 & 16 Dec. 1905.

Small contributions thankfully received.

Erected at the start of the twentieth century, the manse of the Middle St John Church stood on a site facing Glasgow Road on the corner with Murray Place. The bazaar advertised here was intended to raise £1,500 to pay off the debt incurred by the new manse, but only netted £1,080.

FIRE AT CAMPBELL'S DYEWORKS. PERTH. 20 . 19

PULLARS FIRE

Strathtay man Peter Campbell set up in business as a ribbon and garment dyer in Methven Street, near the lade, in 1814. His son, also Peter, learned the dyeing trade in his father's business before going on a working tour that took in London, Paris, Liverpool and Ireland. On his return he formed the partnership of P. & P. Campbell with his father. The business grew and in 1852 moved from Methven Street to a new site next to the lade at St Catherine's Road. The works were extended many times after that, and about 500 agencies were established around the world, but on 20 May 1919 disaster struck. The workforce had left for their lunch break when at about one o'clock smoke was seen coming from the wet cleaning house. Fire brigades hastened to the scene, but by the time they deployed all they could do was limit the fire's spread. Soldiers from the nearby Queen's Barracks also joined the fight and helped to save the Wallace Works across St Catherine's Road. They also removed books and office furniture from P. & P. Campbell's offices, and the household effects of people living in the adjacent Campbell's Buildings, with the result that it looked as if a mass flitting was in progress in Dunkeld Road. Soldiers also emptied the barracks' ammunition magazine, just in case! By five o'clock the fire was spent, leaving a burned-out shell and two large chimneys, one of which still bore the words Perth Dye Works. No lives were lost, but the dream was over and the company was taken over later in the year by its great rivals, Pullar's.

P. & P. Campbell

THE Perth Dye Works

CELEBRATED FOR

Superior Dyeing &
Cleaning of Ladies' &
Gents' Garments,

CURTAINS & OTHER FURNISHINGS

Particulars in Price-List.

From

Edinburgh Receiving Offices,
19, Waterloo Place
(nearly opposite G.P.O.).

31, Newington Road,
3, Viewforth, Bruntsfield, or
1, Royston Terrace, Trinity.

FIRE AT CAMPBELL'S
DYEWORKS. PERTH. 20.5.19

The wreckage of the dye works is seen here beside the lade: water which might have been better used to fight the fire if insurance inspectors, stung by Perth's biggest ever financial fire-loss, were to be believed. They were unsparingly scathing in their criticism of the city's fire-fighting arrangements.

Campbell's great rival, Pullar's, had its own fire brigade. It was often used alongside the city's brigade and set commercial rivalry aside to attend the fire at Campbell's.

39

Perth became a major centre for the dyeing and cleaning business with three large companies based in and around the city: Campbell's; Thomson's (whose works were at Friarton); and Pullar's. The latter was set up by John Pullar in 1824, and like Campbell's used the lade as a source of water and for effluent discharge. Starting with a handful of employees in a couple of rooms, the company grew to occupy a vast site on the corner of Kinnoull and Mill Streets, becoming Perth's largest employer with a workforce of 2,000. It also established numerous agencies, helping it to become an industry leader and a household name throughout the country.

Pullar's purchased the Tulloch Estate in 1882 and erected the largest and most complete dry-cleaning plant in the world there. The Tulloch Works, as it was known, is seen here *c*.1905 behind the Hillyland skating and curling pond with a curling match, or bonspiel, in progress.

Curlers no longer had to wait for the right winter conditions after 1936 when the Perth Ice Rink, in Dunkeld Road, was opened. The facility was also used for other sports like ice hockey, and the Perth Panthers, a professional team, initially consisting of young Canadians but later including local players, became established at the rink. It continued for a time after the Second World War but was unable to keep going financially, and a later attempt to revive the Panthers came to nought. The old rink has also gone, but more modern facilities are available for skaters and curlers at the new Dewar's Ice Rink on the corner of Glasgow Road and Glover Street.

The Woody Islands, just downstream from the Tay's confluence with the River Almond, have long been regarded as a pleasant destination for a riverside walk, a place for men to fish and for boys to play. They featured in a boys' book, *The Young Barbarians*, written by the Revd John Watson under his pen-name Ian MacLaren. One of the islands was also used as the takeoff point for a water supply scheme opened in 1930.

When the tram system was electrified it was also extended along Dunkeld Road to its junction with Crieff Road. Here a tram is passing the large tenement known as Readdie's Buildings and then Hammerman Buildings. It was built in the 1880s, as was Myrtle Place, the terrace in the left foreground.

The Northern District School, on the corner of Dunkeld Road and Muirton Place, was opened in 1910 by Lord Shaw of Dunfermline. It replaced an earlier school which had been the first erected by the school board after it took responsibility for education provision. That school held 580 pupils, but expansion of the area meant that the new school had to cater for 1,130. It comprised twenty classrooms, thirteen of which held 60 senior pupils, the other seven holding 50 infants. There were also cookery and woodwork rooms, and a school garden was laid out in part of the playground. In the 1990s the school pioneered the teaching of Gaelic and started the new millennium with a new name, Balhousie Primary School.

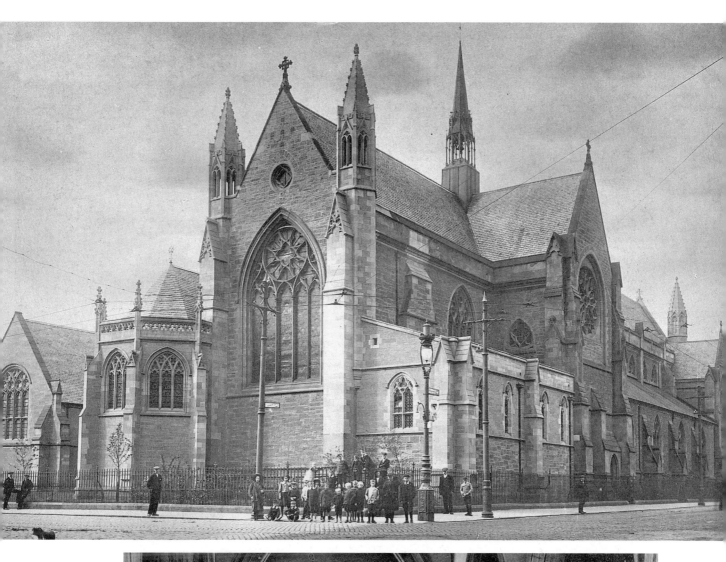

London-based architect William Butterfield was engaged to design the new St Ninian's Episcopal Cathedral on the corner of North Methven and Atholl Streets. Work began in 1849 and by the following year enough of the building had been completed for it to be used for worship. Another phase of building in 1888–90 saw more of the structure

completed, but the partly finished building left problems which had to be resolved by new architects in construction phases between 1901 and 1911, and again in 1939. The east end, seen here both inside and out, was the earliest part of the cathedral to be completed, although the original structure was altered by the addition of hall, chapel, flanking aisle and turrets.

RETREAT HOUSE, PERTH.

The Scottish Episcopalians obtained the lease of Balhousie Castle in 1926 and used it for a number of years as a retreat house, a place where people could spend a few days in peace, quiet and rest. A castle of sorts is thought to have stood on the Balhousie site before it came into the Eviot family in 1422. It changed hands a few times prior to its acquisition by the Hay family, the Earls of Kinnoull. The core of the present building dates from c.1630, although it was heavily modified in 1864 with the addition of turrets and corbeling. The war office used the castle during the Second World War, and after some post-war wrangling regarding its future use it became the regimental headquarters and museum of the Black Watch.

Perth is the home of the Black Watch. The name comes from the regiment's origins as six independent companies set up in 1725 to police the Highlands. Policing in those days was known as 'watching', and the men wore a dark green and black tartan. They were embodied as a regiment in 1740 and despite promises to the contrary were sent overseas. The vacuum created by their absence was filled by the Jacobite rebellion of 1745/46. The transition, however, from police force to military unit set the regiment on a glorious path that has taken it to all the country's major conflicts, most recently in Iraq. With plans afoot to absorb the Scottish infantry regiments into a single unit, the Black Watch is facing a future as a battalion name within the new structure, but its history and associations with Perth can never be erased.

Regiments other than the Black Watch also based themselves at Perth from time to time. Many of these were Territorial Army units which regularly camped in the vicinity of the city in the years before the First World War. These pictures of the Royal Scots Greys and the 18th Hussars were taken *c*.1907.

The army used the North Inch for, amongst other things, the Volunteer Review of 1868 when men showed off their skills and did their best to avoid injuring anyone. This was a different kind of battle from the pointless bloodletting staged in 1396 to settle a clan feud. This trial by combat would no doubt have faded from memory had Sir Walter Scott not included it in his novel the *Fair Maid of Perth*. Watched by King Robert III and his court, 30 men from each of Clan Chattan and Clan Kay assembled to fight to the death. One man came to his senses and swam across the Tay to escape. His place was taken by local armourer, Hal o' the Wynd, who, unlike most of the clansmen, survived the carnage.

Sporting battles have also long been a feature of the Inch, with football, rugby and horse-racing all taking place there. Perthshire Cricket Club plays on the Inch, even hosting (and losing to) the mighty Australians. Golf too has a long history on the Inch, although these folk on the putting green, and those watching them make a hash of it, are enjoying a less serious form of hitting a ball into a hole.

Rowing and other forms of boating have also been part of the recreational life of the Inch.

The North Inch was also used for practical activities like bleaching and hanging out washing and grazing cattle, but in more recent times its attractions have been tailored more to people's enjoyment of the pleasant parkland beside the Tay. In summer there were shows to watch – Dave Dunlop's Entertainers (illustrated here) appeared in Perth in 1910, and although it is not known where they performed they were the kind of troupe that would have graced the stage occupied by the Perth Pierrots to the left of the Perthshire Volunteers' monument. A variety of caterers selling their wares from carts and barrows appear in photographs of the Inches, although the ice cream seller in the lower picture from the 1920s has dispensed with the kind of canopy used by many of the earlier vendors.

Fair Maid's House, Perth

The survival of the building known as the Fair Maid's House has a lot to do with Sir Walter Scott selecting it as the home of Catherine Glover, the central character in the *Fair Maid of Perth*. In doing so he employed a grand literary tradition of not letting the truth get in the way of a good story, because the book is set in 1396 and the building's known life starts in 1629 when it was bought by the Glovers Incorporation of Perth, who used it as a meeting house for 150 years. Heavy-handed restoration in the 1890s left little of the original intact, but it survived to become a valuable tourist attraction. The adjacent building known as the townhouse of Lord John Murray has also survived from the early eighteenth century, although altered by restoration.

The altar, Fair Maid's House.

Rose Terrace is in effect two terraces of townhouses with the former Perth Academy building sandwiched between them. Construction of the houses began before the school, which was built in 1803–04 to the designs of architect Robert Reid. Although this picture was used as a postcard in the early twentieth century, it appears to have been taken before 1886 when a clock and statue of Britannia were added to the parapet above the main entrance to the school. In the distance, facing the camera, is Barossa Place.

Completing a run of Georgian elegance between Rose Terrace and the bridge are Atholl Crescent and Atholl Place, and if they enjoy splendid views across the North Inch then the view of them from the Inch must be one of the country's finest townscapes. The middle picture, taken from Rose Terrace, has just caught the end of Atholl Crescent on the right. The lower picture shows Atholl Place looking back toward Rose Terrace.

When the bridge linking Perth with the other side of Tay was swept away in 1621 it was the latest in a long line of failures, and the good folk of Perth must have wondered if the swift-flowing river could ever be successfully bridged. Their confidence must indeed have taken a knock, because almost 150 years passed before funds for a new bridge could be raised, and in the meantime those wanting to cross the river had to use a ferry. Perth took no chances with its new bridge and engaged John Smeaton, a man of proven ability, to design it. He was regarded as the father of civil engineering, a term he devised himself to distinguish what he did from military engineers, and he carried out some spectacular work including the building of the Eddystone Lighthouse and the Forth & Clyde Canal. Smeaton's Perth Bridge was a masterpiece, not just strong and functional but elegantly beautiful too. Its opening in 1771 acted as a catalyst for the regeneration of the city – a phrase modern town planners would readily understand.

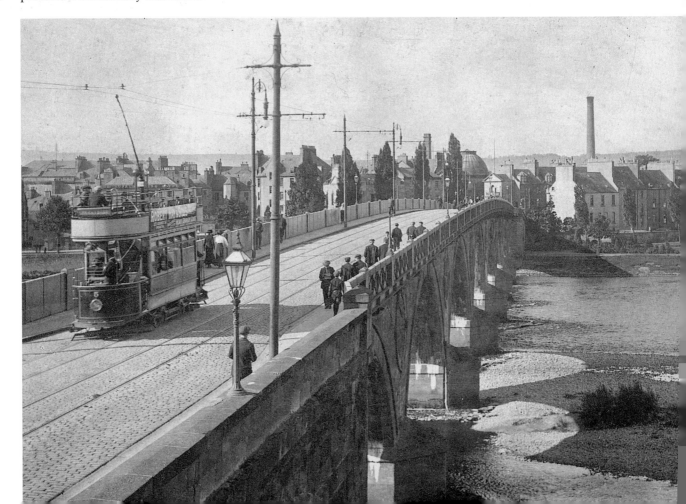

George Street, created to give access to and from the bridge, was of course lined with new buildings. One of these was the post office, strategically sited for the mail coaches using the new route. Across the street was another new building, the George Inn, built to capitalise on the trade brought by that coaching traffic. The city's older inns were not so well placed as this newcomer, which rapidly grew in status, and then following an unexpected visit from Queen Victoria leapt to the level of being 'Royal'. Known since as the Royal George Hotel, it also scored over the older city inns by having an outlook across the river, something no other competitor could offer.

The tolbooth, which ran across the eastern end of High Street (see page 6), was where civic affairs were conducted until a fire in 1834. This gave the council the opportunity to clear the area, open up High Street to the river and adapt what remained on the site as a council chamber and burgh court room. This was completed in 1840, but councillors soon became concerned about the condition of the cells and the prospect of losing government policing grants if these were not improved. They decided to demolish the old building (illustrated here) and replace it.

The new municipal buildings were opened in 1879. There was an entrance from High Street which led by a spacious stair to the council chamber, committee room, town clerk's office and lord provost's room. Another entrance from Tay Street led to offices for the chamberlain and the police, with eight cells on the ground floor and the police court above. The adjacent site in Tay Street was also developed for the fire department and to provide offices and a house for the superintendent of police. Superintendent Buist was on duty on the morning of 23 January 1895 when at about three o'clock he thought the chimney in the police office was on fire, but soon discovered that the sparks falling into the fireplace were coming from a more serious outbreak. The fire destroyed the upper floor containing the council chamber and police court, along with many of the contents. The buildings were later restored and extended further up High Street.

Tay Street was not developed until the nineteenth century, before which the grounds of large houses ran down to the river, blocking public access to the water's edge. The grandest of these was the Gowrie House which belonged to the Earls of Gowrie. While a guest there in 1600, King James VI was heard to shout 'murder', and his courtiers, in rushing to defend him, killed the 3rd Earl and his brother, the Master of Gowrie. Their deaths are the only certainty in a murky tale of plot and counter-plot that has never been satisfactorily explained, and the house took its secrets with it when it was cleared away for the Tay Street buildings. The sheriff court, the building with the classical pediment in the distance, was built on the site between 1819 and 1822 and is still in use, whereas the Baptist Church, with its distinctive square tower, was destroyed by fire in 1984.

The Scottish Girls' Friendly Society offered a place for young women to meet and make friends in a secure and friendly environment. Its headquarters were in Edinburgh and there was a network of branches in Scotland and abroad. The Perth lodge, known as Riverside House, was at 72 Tay Street and was gifted by Sir Robert Pullar in 1887. It offered hostel accommodation for up to ten girls and had rooms where members could congregate and relax. All meetings ended with Bible lessons and prayer.

The city's Black Maria is seen here outside the municipal buildings, which housed the police court and cells. There were other cells further along Tay Street at the sheriff court, and of course a whole prisonful of them a bit further south. It is likely therefore that this vehicle ferried customers around between all three, and clearly attracted a more positive level of public support than the politically charged attention given to prisoner escort services today. The term Black Maria is said to owe its origins to a mid-nineteenth century black woman, Maria Lee, who kept a boarding house in Boston, USA, and helped police in escorting drunk and disorderly customers to jail.

Perth's fire brigade is seen here outside the county buildings: a note with the picture describes it as having been taken in 1909 on the day the foundation stone for the new city hall was laid. Alas the civic pride evident here took a severe knock ten years later, when after the fire at Campbell's Dye Works in May 1919 (see pages 38 and 39), insurance inspectors described the fire engine as 'primitive and ineffective', a 'wretched toy' and a 'disgrace to the city'.

The number of road crossings over the river at Perth was doubled in 1900 when Victoria Bridge was built. A couple of houses on the Kinnoull side were half-demolished to make way for its construction and became known as the 'twa gables'!

The original Victoria Bridge, seen here during an intense frost in January 1918, was replaced by an elegant concrete structure in 1960. It was named Queen's Bridge in honour of Queen Elizabeth, who opened it with the same pair of scissors that had been used to open Victoria Bridge. The Queen's visit, the first to the city by a reigning monarch since 1914, was of particular significance as it was the year in which Perth celebrated its 750th anniversary as a royal burgh.

The view from the railway bridge has become an almost iconic image of Perth. It is seen here in the late 1870s before Victoria Bridge was built.

Dredging sand in the Tay had the double benefit of keeping the shipping channel clear and providing a useful building material. Here a cart has been taken down the slipway beside the railway bridge to unload a sand barge. The way the pole, or perhaps the mast has been shoved through the railings may be unconventional, but was no doubt a tried and tested method of holding the boat steady.

The Dundee & Perth Railway was opened in 1847. It was the first to serve the city, although its initial terminus was at Barnhill and passengers had to complete their journey over the river by other means. This situation prevailed for two years while a curving bridge was built across the river and over Moncrieffe Island. It was made of wooden arches resting on stone pillars and incorporated a swing section to allow shipping to continue up to the city quays. The demise of this traffic allowed the bridge to be replaced in 1862 by the present structure. The line then terminated just beyond the bridge, but was extended to the main Perth Station in 1886. The old station was renamed Princes Street.

The city's water supply was replaced in 1830–32 by a well sunk on Moncrieffe Island. This filtered water through natural gravel and it was then piped to the domed waterworks structure which can be seen above the railway bridge. The ornate chimney was for a steam engine which pumped the water up into a holding tank. The system was superseded in 1965 and the redundant building was converted for use as a gallery celebrating the work of the artist J. D. Ferguson.

A pedestrian walkway beside the railway bridge ended Moncrieffe Island's island status and allowed it to be used for allotment gardens and the King James VI golf course. The clubhouse is seen here, raised on a mound to protect it from flooding.

South Inch.

Many, many thanks for P.C. Your devoted Charles

We have had a "flood" all to ourselves here; otherwise "swimmingly."

This is where you stood to hear "Pastor Primmer".

The South Inch does not run down to the river's edge like the North Inch, but on occasions the river has risen to meet it, as in January 1903 when the writer of this postcard likened it to a biblical flood. Heavy rain, combined with strong winds and melting snow, caused the flood which covered the Inch and the Edinburgh Road. People living in Marshall Place had to enter and leave their houses through the back doors.

Water on the South Inch was not confined to floods – people could take to a boat on the boating pond, or sail their own model yacht on the placid waters.

Before it moved to Ingliston near Edinburgh, the Highland & Agricultural Society Show (now the Royal Highland Show) was held at a number of locations around the country. It first came to Perth in 1829 and returned at regular intervals, with its ninth visit in July 1904 when the show was held on the South Inch. Twenty-seven special trains brought thousands of people to enjoy the exhibits and competitions, drink aerated water, eat strawberries or take tea in the temperance tent. Entertainment was provided by itinerant musicians whose ranks, according to the *Perthshire Advertiser*, were made up largely of 'disabled seamen or dismembered colliers'(!). Takings at the gate over the four days exceeded all but one of the previous ten shows, and that was an exceptional event in Edinburgh in 1899 attended by the Prince of Wales.

Catering at the Highland Show and for other events on the South Inch was provided by mobile drinks vendors, although whether this one is selling aerated water or something stronger is not known. Wright's Perth Brewery – 'There's Nothing Wrong with Wright's' – was latterly located at the South Inch before it closed in the early 1960s.

Marshall Place was designed by Robert Reid in 1801 as the southern flank of Perth's new town, but although the Georgian terraces are splendid the crowning architectural glory is Victorian: St Leonard's in the Fields Free Church with its crown spire. It was built in 1885 for a congregation that broke away from St Leonard's Parish Church in King Street in 1843. They worshipped for some years in Victoria Street (see page 23) before the architect John James Stevenson, a London-based Scot with a strong commitment to the Free Church, designed their new building.

Facing the South Inch from the elevated vantage point of St Leonard's Bank is a row of individually designed villas dating from the early nineteenth century. The one seen here is No. 7.

One of Perth's early photographers was Magnus Jackson, who initially worked out of a studio in Marshall Place. He took a series of pictures published as 'Perth's Old Worthies' by J. K. Taylor *c*.1905. Although interesting, these images were in reality of society's less fortunate members who were often mentally handicapped. Pate Ostler was a small-time horse dealer who sold coal from his cart. Blue Caum Kate acquired her unwanted nickname by selling the chalky substance used to whiten or colour doorsteps. Buckie Gray also disliked his nickname, with which ignorant youngsters taunted him. The railway authorities allowed him to act as a station porter, without officially employing him – hence the uniform. Jock Salmon was a bad-smelling individual who wandered around doing odd jobs, and Whistling Willie (bottom right) was always counting the days to an annual dinner he was entitled to.

The speed with which public railways developed during the nineteenth century gave communities like Perth little time to adjust to a new phenomenon that could transform their fortunes. In the mid-1840s the Scottish Central Railway and other companies were pressing for a site to build a station and marshalling yards. The South Inch was proposed, but that idea was dropped in favour of the present location. The first train arrived in 1848 and soon others were converging from all directions, making Perth a major railway hub. The station was expanded many times to keep up with demand and is seen here early in the twentieth century: the interior view of the main concourse shows the fruit stall and vendors who have basketwork trays around their necks so that they can cater for passengers on trains. The exterior view shows a train heading south on the main line.

The train leaving the station in the middle picture is being hauled by one of a new class of locomotives introduced in 1906 by the North British Railway. These were known as 'Atlantics', because of their wheel arrangement, and were given names to reflect the routes they were intended to run on. *Liddesdale*, seen here at Perth yard, may have been operating out of her area because the Atlantics proved too heavy for the Waverley line south of Edinburgh and had to be redeployed. The locomotive on the right of the picture is Caledonian Railway No. 484, which was built in the 1870s to haul goods traffic and converted in

1886 for use on passenger trains.

Perth Station was invaded annually by people heading for the hills to hunt, shoot and fish. At the start and finish of the season the Highland Railway's trains were full of people, luggage, dogs and all the paraphernalia of the sporting estate. Hauling these heavy trains over the distance and gradients to Inverness was hard work and the Highland Railway designed special locomotives to do it. The one seen here leaving Perth Station for the north is *Loch Naver*, one of a class of fifteen introduced in 1896. They were amongst the most powerful locomotives in the country at the time – the louvres in the funnel were designed to create an updraught to lift the smoke clear of the driving cab windows.

Perth is familiar with floods from the Tay, but the inundation of July 1916 was different. Drains and sewers were unable to cope with the volume of rain that fell continuously for 48 hours and areas which were normally high and dry were swamped. Over two feet of water covered the railway running north out of the station, forcing officials to limit operations to a single track for safety. People who lined the Glasgow Road bridge to watch trains plough through the flood declared that they had never seen anything like it.

This locomotive, standing at the platform for Dundee, was a one-off built by Neilson & Co. of Glasgow to show off their wares at the Edinburgh Exhibition of 1886. After that she was bought by the Caledonian Railway and given the number 123. She proved to be highly effective and was used for many years as a pilot engine for royal trains. In 1923 the Caledonian was absorbed into the London, Midland & Scottish Railway (LMS) who gave the engine the new number seen in this picture. She was not scrapped when she was withdrawn in 1935 and is now preserved (as CR 123) in Glasgow's Museum of Transport. The former Station Hotel in the background also had royal connections.

In the days when everybody travelled by rail, every major railway centre had a large hotel in close proximity to the station. Railway hotels catered primarily for well-to-do passengers and for Perth's Station Hotel none was more prestigious than Queen Victoria, who stopped off there for something to eat on her journeys to and from Balmoral. Where a single railway operator worked the station they usually built the hotel and named it after the company, but with Perth Station being operated jointly the hotel was also a shared venture, built in 1888. Changing times mean that the building still exists but under another name.

Leonard Street was graced by two other large hotels whose names, the Royal British and the Queen's, also hinted at royal patronage. The Queen's was the larger of the two with 50 bedrooms. It offered patrons a 'private room for meetings' and catered for wedding parties which, because it was a temperance hotel, would not have been the drink-fuelled rammies so characteristic of such occasions.

THE ROYAL BRITISH HOTEL, PERTH

TELEPHONE NO. 315.

The Royal British Hotel had half the number of bedrooms as the Queen's, but was in a prime position facing the station. It might almost have been put there deliberately, but was actually a late eighteenth century building that predated the railway.

The Atholl Private Hotel on St Leonard's Bank was also in a good position to pick up railway trade. It had twelve bedrooms and could offer private gardens plus fine views across the South Inch. Allied to a combination of 'moderate terms' and 'home baking', this gave it a winning formula. It is still a hotel.

St Leonard's Bridge, which spanned the railway tracks to the south of the station, linked the city centre with Craigie, a district which grew rapidly in the late nineteenth century. One of its principal thoroughfares, Abbott Street, is seen here from the bridge, with Priory Place on the left.

This view of Abbot Street shows it looking back toward the bridge. Craigie School, in the left foreground, was originally built by Perth School Board in 1884 as the Western District Public School and had its name changed to the one everyone used in 1953. In the middle distance is a large building erected by the City of Perth Co-operative Society in 1890. The society itself was formed in 1871 with 90 members, £85 capital and annual sales of £704. It thrived until the decline of the co-operative movement in the 1960s. The ground floor shop is now a pub which shares the name Abbotsford with the tenement flats across the road.

The Co-op building in Abbot Street is seen facing the camera in this view of Friar Street from Queen Street. Like the Co-op, most of the houses on the left were late nineteenth century structures, but Crichton Place, the block of tenement flats on the right, was not built until 1905.

The houses at the southern end of Wilson Street also date mostly from the late nineteenth century, as does Craigie Parish Church, at the top of the hill, which was built in 1894/95 as St Stephen's Church. In the 1920s a pair of cottages was erected diagonally opposite the church by the builders Soutar & McQueen. One of them, Ingleknowe, was where the poet William Soutar, the son of one of the builders, lived out his days after contracting an illness while serving in the navy during the First World War. By 1930 he was confined to bed in a room adapted to give him a view of the garden. He worked there until his death in 1943.

The curving line of Wilson Street, with Craigie Parish Church at its crest, can be seen in this view looking across the mill building roofs and the valley of the Craigie Burn. The back gardens of the houses in Queen Street can be seen beyond the roofs in the foreground.

The dramatic falls at Craigie were almost tailor-made for mills to be erected below them.

Windsor Terrace is seen here behind the bridge carrying Glenearn Road over the Craigie Burn. The road has now been widened and the bridge rebuilt with a concrete deck and metal railings instead of the stone walls and arch seen in the foreground. This was the terminus for the Craigie trams, and their overhead electric cables can be seen on the right running up to the two upright poles beside the bridge.

W. L. Hanson, the same local photographer who took the picture above, appears to have walked the few yards between that view and this (or maybe between this view and that!) to take this picture of Queen Street from the point where Glenearn Road becomes the southern continuation of Priory Place.

To the south of Craigie is the more suburban Craigie Road, seen here from the garden of No. 27 looking across at No. 28. Friarton Hill can be seen in the distance.

Friarton Hill is a good vantage point from which to view Perth. This 1930s picture and its neighbour on the facing page were taken from the same spot at the same time, giving a (slightly distorted) panoramic view of the city. Edinburgh Road is seen on the left cradling the Friarton housing scheme and curving toward the South Inch. In the left middle-distance is Craigie Road, the first built-up area beyond open ground which has since been developed with buildings as well as a new road layout. The railway yards on the right have been replaced by the Tesco supermarket.

This older view, taken in 1878, shows the Edinburgh Road tollhouse in the foreground with the railway bridge and harbour beyond. Perth's harbour moved progressively downriver over the centuries as the Tay silted up and boats got bigger. The original harbour, opposite the end of High Street, was eventually superseded by the widened and deepened section of the lade, where Canal Street is now, and a coal harbour at the mouth of the lade. Friarton had become established as the harbour by 1854 when an Act of Parliament authorised its enlargement and improvement. It all helped to make the Tay the nearest thing in Scotland to the river navigations of Europe, where many of the ships now calling at Perth come from.

The harbour, with associated industries, can also be seen in this view from Friarton Hill looking across the housing scheme. In common with towns and cities across the country, Perth responded to the housing Acts of 1919, 1924 and 1930 which authorised councils to build and manage municipal houses. Hitherto housing had rarely been provided by public authorities, so this was a new area of activity for councils. Nevertheless Perth had built about 440 houses by the early 1930s when it embarked on its largest scheme to date, at Friarton, where 226 homes were planned.

These two steam lighters have been photographed on the river downstream of the harbour at Friarton, but it is difficult to be certain what they are doing. They don't look to be underway and one appears to have a mooring line out, yet they have steam up at the foredeck winches. The most likely guess is that they are dredging for sand. The rowing boat in the foreground is a curiosity – it has only one rower, but two sets of oars – which suggests it was used by the photographer to get to the ideal spot for the picture.

Shamrock operated as a pleasure steamer on the Tay between 1905 and 1909. She is seen here passing the gasworks which was established at Friarton in 1901 to replace the former works in Canal Street. On the hillside above the gasworks is the fever or infectious diseases hospital, built at Friarton by Perth Corporation and opened by Sir Robert Pullar in late October 1906. It had 36 beds for people suffering from ailments like typhoid fever, diphtheria and scarlet fever. The NHS used the building for tuberculosis patients and called it Friarton Hospital. It closed in 1959 and reopened as a detention centre in 1963.

It took three years – from 1845 to 1848 – for the Scottish Central Railway to drive the 1,220-yard Moncrieffe Tunnel through the hills to the south of Perth and get their tracks into the city. Parliamentary approval was also given to the Edinburgh & Northern Railway to join the Scottish Central's tracks at Hilton Junction and run through the tunnel to Perth General Station. The tunnel engineers initially thought that the rock was sound enough to stand without a lining, but the action of water and locomotive fumes caused it to deteriorate. Work to line the tunnel started in 1901 and lasted for three years. The rails were relaid as a single track down the centre so that trains could still operate while the work went on around them. This framework, known as centring, was used to support the six layers of brickwork while they were being laid. It is seen here from the southern portal at Craigend.

Craigend occupies a lovely spot on a south-facing slope with fine views of Strathearn, but has also proved attractive to those developing Perth's transport routes. Moncrieffe Tunnel runs directly below the hamlet (which sits above its southern portal), but if passing trains disturbed the peace the impact of roads has been infinitely more dramatic. Motorways now converge on it from three directions and, along with the old main road, form a four-way high-level interchange. For many drivers therefore Craigend is the name of a road junction and looks very different from this century-old image of a little cottage and its splendid tree.

The railway companies were amongst the biggest employers in Perth, providing work for something in excess of 2,000 people, many of whom lived right beside their work in Glover Street. Some of the old houses remain, although the curved stairs giving access to these upper flats have now been straightened out. Transport still has an impact on the street, which has become an unofficial city centre bypass, resulting in the old cobbled road surface being replaced by modern traffic calming measures. Many of today's drivers would no doubt love to see the road as empty as this.

Kinfauns Crescent in Needless Road is seen here from the end of Darnhall Drive where, in 1920, Perth Corporation erected its first council houses. That initial scheme was for sixteen homes, but ten years later the total number of council houses built or being constructed in the area amounted to 250.

Many of those houses built in the Darnhall Drive area can be seen from Craigie Hill golf course, which also gives splendid views across the city from the south-west. The course was opened in 1911 with access from Cherrybank.

Pitheavlis Castle, an L-shaped laird's house, appears to have been built in the late sixteenth century by a Robert Stewart after he bought the lands from John Ross of Craigie. It passed through a succession of owners, but was described in the late nineteenth century as 'partly inhabited as a farm house' and 'does not appear to be well maintained or cared for'. It is now looked after by Perth & Kinross Council and used as flats. The picture shows the original house with a turreted square stair tower to the right, and to the left a two-storey wing dating from the seventeenth century. The top of a circular stair tower can just be seen above its roof.

Cherrybank was an independent village a mile out of Perth on Glasgow Road until it was absorbed by the growing city. That growth was stimulated by the tram service to and from Scone. Initially the horse-drawn trams only came up Glasgow Road as far as Rose Crescent, but the tracks were extended to Cherrybank in 1898.

The introduction of trams to Cherrybank meant that the lovely wooded glen known as the Buckie Braes was brought within everyone's reach. It was developed as parkland by Perth Corporation before the First World War – this picture shows the entrance.

The children's playground was highly regarded with its seesaw, swings and maypole, a death-defying apparatus which would doubtless find little favour in today's health and safety conscious climate.

Amongst the 'Buckies' many attractions were picnic places with open fireplaces and grills where a pot could be boiled to make tea. These secluded spots were also ideal for romantic trysts.

The old main road to Perth from the south-west ran along Strathearn and approached the city by way of Aberdalgie and Necessity Brae. This somewhat strenuous route was superseded by the present Glasgow Road coming in by way of Broxden. The two roads converged at Cherrybank with the old road, now known as Low Road, rising steeply to (or falling sharply away from) the junction with the new. A line of buildings including this post office made the most of this situation, with their lower floors facing Low Road and their upper floors fronting the higher-level Glasgow Road.

The old post office can be seen on the right of this view of Glasgow Road looking back toward the city. Oakbank Road can just be discerned joining the main road on the left between the tenement block and the shop with the extended awning. There have been a number of alterations to the buildings since the picture was taken c.1906, but some things don't change – youngsters from Perth Academy, like the children in the picture, gather every lunchtime to avail themselves of the goodies on offer at the new post office-cum-general store which has been built alongside the old one.

The development of Cherrybank and the surrounding area is shown clearly by the pictures on these two pages. This one was used as a postcard in 1913 by a woman who relates a meeting with her friend Andrew. They boarded a tram at Bridgend and went to the Buckie Braes for a picnic: 'Andrew was fair taken up with Cherrybank' she says. The Cherrybank Inn can be seen just to the right of centre with gardens on the sloping ground to the front and rear. The inn, which dates from 1761, was well-placed to provide refreshment to carters driving horse-hauled vehicles over the braes to Strathearn. The postcard writer has also put a cross on a house on the extreme right of the picture. The same house has been ringed on the picture on the right to assist identification.

The trees on the left of the picture above are masking Cleeve, a large country house where these historically attired people took part in a fete in 1920 to raise funds for St Ninian's Cathedral and its foreign missions. Local people dressed in the costumes of royalty from four historical periods paraded round the grounds and then sat in regal splendour while a 'courier' read a proclamation encouraging all attendees to loosen their purse strings and aid the good causes. This group represented King James I (Mr Crawford), his queen (Morna McGregor), a courier (David Martin), two pages (the Misses Hall) and five retainers (names not known). Since the Second World War Cleeve has been used as a children's home, an agricultural college, a caravan site and now housing.

In 1932 Perth Academy left its cramped premises in Rose Terrace (see page 49) and moved to spacious new buildings on the elevated site seen here at Viewlands. The resiting of the school at this location inevitably encouraged the building of many new houses nearby. It was not the first school in the area: on the extreme right of the picture and marked with an arrow is the little Cherrybank School, which was begun by the Cherrybank, Burghmuir, Pitheavlis and Upper and Lower Craigie School Society which raised the funds to have the school built in 1865. It was taken over by the school board after the Education Act of 1872.

PERTH ACADEMICALS R.U.F.C.

The Academy's former pupils formed Perth Academicals Rugby Union Football Club in 1929 and won the Midlands seven-a-side tournament cup in season 1934/35. The full fifteen-a-side team played in the Midland League. They are:
Back row: A. Guild, R. Halley, L. McLean, J. Kinnear, J. Darling, J. Herd, J. Douglas, A. Robertson, J. Riach, A. Douglas
Front row: W. Gilmour, I. Hamilton, J. Flight (captain), E. Sturrock, A. Clark
The club amalgamated with Perthshire RFC in 1947.

Huntingtower, seat of the influential Ruthven family, was initially made up of two fifteenth-century towers built just over nine feet apart. This gap became known as the Maiden's Leap when, to avoid being discovered in a secret tryst with her socially inferior lover, a daughter of the 1st Earl of Gowrie is reputed to have leapt from one rooftop to the other. About 100 years after the young lady's desperate measure a building was erected between the two towers creating a single unified structure. In the early twentieth century, when panelling and plaster were removed from inside the castle, some remarkable early decoration was revealed including a complete painted ceiling in the east tower, the one closest to the camera here.

A twenty-room mansion, also known as Huntingtower, was situated due east of the castle. Formerly the property of the Lindsay-Mercer family, it was empty and owned by a Mr Swan when the town council purchased it and the 21-acre estate. The house was demolished in the autumn of 1956 and the crematorium built on the site.

The Perth, Almond Valley & Methven Railway was opened in 1858 and was later extended beyond Methven to Crieff. It branched off the main line about a mile and a half north of Perth Station and headed west past Huntingtower where this little station, known as Ruthven Road, served the local community until services were withdrawn in 1951.

Crieff Road, seen here at the intersection with Tulloch Terrace, is wider now and traffic lights control the junction. The building in the left foreground has gone and the almost rural appearance of the surrounding area has been transformed by the Letham and Tulloch council housing estates. Pullar's began the process of change when they built their Tulloch Works on the old country estate of the same name (see page 40), but now that too has gone and amongst recent nearby developments is McDiarmid Park, home of Perth's senior football team, St Johnstone.

We think of football as our national game, but up to the late nineteenth century organised sports were largely confined to the summer months with cricket, rowing and golf amongst the most popular. Football began to grow in Perth following a meeting held in 1884 with the aim of developing the game as a winter sport. First in the field was Pullar's Rangers, which was made up mainly of company employees. They were followed by St Johnstone, a team of bankers, clerks and doctors; a railwaymen's team known as Caledonian; Erin Rovers, a team with Irish connections; and Fair City Athletic. This team disappeared for a time, but reformed in 1934 and is seen here after winning the Perthshire Senior League in 1936.

FAIR CITY ATHLETIC F.C.

The Perth League, initially made up of five teams, was one of the earliest in Scotland. It ceased playing in 1914 when war broke out, with some of those early teams surviving while others disappeared and new teams like Craigie FC (illustrated here) appeared. The most notable survivor is, of course, St Johnstone, which was admitted to the Scottish League in 1911.

The Half-Holiday League played on those midweek days when shops closed in the afternoon, so people called them the 'shopkeepers'.

Perth Roselea was formed in the 1890s and the team are seen here in the 1930s when they played in the Perth & District Junior League.

Back row: J. Gregor, A. Stewart, L. Smith, J. Donaldson (Capt.), J. Christie, J. McLeish.

Front row: J. McKerchar, H. Thomson, I. Gray, J. Christie, G. McLagan.

Perth Celtic continued the Irish tradition, begun by Erin Rovers. Like Roselea they played in the Perth & District Junior League and are seen here in the 1930s.

Back row: F. Robertson, T. McFarlane, J. Miller, A. Gregor, J. Duncan (Capt.), J. McFarlane.

Front row: R. Ferguson, D. Elder, J. McIntosh, T. Carsill, J. Brown

A Perth photographer took this picture of what appears to be a boys' or youth team, but sadly neither he nor anyone else recorded the team name on it.

85

A woman washing clothes outside her cottage offers a different image of Quarrymill to that of today. It also differs from the former industrial scene of quarrying and milling that this lovely wooded glen of the Annaty Burn is named after. It is now laid out as a woodland park belonging to the Gannochy Trust, which was founded by Arthur Kinmond Bell of Bell's Whisky.

When the Scone & Perth Omnibus Company began operating horse-drawn buses between Scone and Perth in the 1860s they also stimulated a growth in house building. Many fine villas had been erected in Pitcullen Crescent by 1894 when the Perth & District Tramway Co. took over the bus company and began running trams the following year. Perth Town Council bought the tramway company in 1903 and introduced electric trams in 1905: here one of these runs along Pitcullen Crescent with a horse-drawn tram behind, indicating that the picture was taken at the time of transition between the two systems. Housing development continued in the late 1920s and early 1930s when Arthur Bell & Sons built 150 houses at Gannochy. The scheme became known as the 'sunshine suburb' because each house was aligned to face the sun.

If people called the little village on the east bank of the river Bridgend when there was no bridge, it was something of a misnomer because the inhabitants spent much of their time ferrying others to and from Perth. The opening of the bridge in 1771 brought all that to an end, and Bridgend grew from a down-at-heel collection of thatched cottages into a sizeable community. The high level of the new bridge meant that the riverside road had to be realigned, so Main Street (illustrated here) is a post-bridge creation, as are Gowrie and Dundee Roads through Kinnoull and Barnhill.

A tram from Scone turns the corner from Main Street into Bridge Street, with East Bridge Street ascending the brae in the background. At the end of the bridge parapet on the right is the old toll house. The collection of tolls had ceased some time before the advent of the trams and when this picture was taken the building was being used by fruiterer, fishmonger and poulterer J. I. Laing. He offered fruits in season, had daily deliveries of fresh or cured fish and gave all orders 'personal attention'.

Inchbank House, a large Georgian villa in Bridgend's Main Street, is seen from the rear on the right of this view looking upstream from the bridge. The other villas in the picture, with garden ground running down to the river, were built in Isla Road (the road to Old Scone) in the late eighteenth and early nineteenth centuries. They start from the appropriately named Newlands, to the left of Inchbank, and run to the turreted Tayside, half-hidden by trees on the left of the picture. The same house is also seen on the facing page. The site on the right below Inchbank was developed for housing in the 1970s.

This tower was built as a riverside gazebo and boathouse for Springland, a house in Isla Road which dates from c.1790.

Tayside, the imposing Isla Road home of Sir Robert (inset) and Lady Pullar, has now been demolished, with only the gateposts remaining. Sir Robert was the eldest son of John Pullar, founder of the Pullar's of Perth dyeing and cleaning business. He became Lord Provost of Perth and its MP, and used his wealth to support many good causes.

Bridgend, downstream of the bridge, seen from the west bank of the river.

Mayfield is a large house in Gannochy Road, opposite the entrance to the Murray Royal Hospital. In the early 1900s, when this picture was probably taken, it belonged to a Blackfriars Street solicitor, John G. Millar. The large garden where these children played is now the site of private houses.

Bowerswell Road is seen in this *c.*1905 picture at the point where it divides, with one branch (right) going on up to Corsie and Kinnoull Hills and the other leading to a number of large villas including Bowerswell House. The house was almost exactly 100 years old when it was taken over by the town council and opened as a home for the elderly as a memorial to those who had lost their lives during the Second World War.

Opposite: The backs of properties in Commercial Street can be seen in this view looking across the river. Just left of centre is Fenwick's Kinnoull Bakery, which supplied the firm's city centre tea rooms, one of which, in County Place, is seen on page 30.

This view from the bridge shows the Tay as it flows between Stanners Island and Bridgend. It also shows, slightly left of centre, the end of a ferry slipway which was on the line of the bridge that was swept away in 1621. The buildings seen here running down to the water's edge were in the old low-lying riverside road known as Commercial Street. It remained a thriving thoroughfare for 200 years after the bridge was opened, but was cleared away in 1975 to make way for a housing development which has transformed this view. One of the few remaining landmarks is Kinnoull Church, in the distance beside the poplar trees.

Kinnoull Church, seen here on the left, was erected in the 1820s to the designs of architect William Burn. It sits directly opposite Kinnoull Primary School which was built 50 years later. This early twentieth century view looking north along the Dundee Road to Bridgend has changed little, although the eight-storey Potterhill Flats, erected in 1960/61, now protrude above the trees on the right. The old sixteenth-century parish church, situated a little to the south, was demolished about ten years after completion of the new church. An aisle which formed part of the church, and which contains a remarkable monument to the 1st Earl of Kinnoull, was retained and is now open to the public.

The old Kinnoull Parish Church stood just out of shot to the left of this early twentieth century picture, taken from the railway bridge. Kinnoull, like Bridgend and Barnhill, grew from being an insubstantial, separate community into part of a continuous development on the east bank of the river when the bridge in effect made all three part of Perth. Businesses like the nurseries seen in the foreground here were established soon after completion of the bridge, but the principal development was in upmarket housing. St Mary's Monastery, high on the hillside, was another post-bridge development.

Opposite: Although many of these buildings have been altered and others added, the hamlet of Corsiehill still retains the general appearance it had when this picture was taken early in the twentieth century. Situated in relative isolation, but close to the city and on ancient routes across the hills, its residents in times past are reputed to have supplemented their income with the proceeds of smuggling.

The Congregation of the Most Holy Redeemer was founded in Italy in 1732 by St Alphonsus Ligouri. The aim of the Redemptorists, as they were also known, was to live together as a Christian community, constantly renewing their dedication to the Lord and the priesthood so that they could take the gospel out into the world to people who for one reason or another were not in a position to either hear it or accept it. Another significant early figure in the congregation was Edward Douglas, a Scot who gave money to the order and spent his working life with it in Rome. It was therefore fitting that as the Redemptorists began to establish a worldwide network they should seek to build a monastery in Scotland. Perth was quickly chosen as the location and work on St Mary's Monastery at Kinnoull was begun in March 1868. It was completed the following year, and celebrated its centenary in 1969 with an open-air mass attended by 500 people.

Interior St Mary's, Kinnoull, Perth

This group of humble dwellings along the Dundee Road was about all there was of Barnhill before the area began to be seen as a desirable place to build large and expensive houses. The garden of one such house, now a hotel, is in the left foreground of this early twentieth century picture, but the area is better known for another garden, Branklyn, a beautiful oasis now in the care of the National Trust for Scotland. The buildings on the right are part of Hillside Home.

A charitable body, the Society for Relief of Incurables in Perth and Perthshire, held a fund-raising bazaar in December 1875 and used the money to set up the Hillside Home. Patients who gained admittance to the home were suffering from cancer and other chronic diseases and conditions from which they were not expected to recover. Hillside gave them a form of sanctuary where they could live out their lives making craft items which were sold to provide funds for the society, which also expected patients' relatives to help pay for accommodation – such was the precarious nature of funding for this unglamorous area of health care before the National Health Service was set up in 1948. Under the NHS the home was renamed Hillside Hospital and remained in use until December 1997.

A rise in the number of people suffering from tuberculosis toward the end of the nineteenth century prompted the society to seek additional funding to provide care for those with TB in a separate building. The principal donors were Sir Robert and Lady Pullar, who gave £10,000 toward the establishment of a sanatorium. This was opened in 1901 on a splendid elevated site overlooking the Tay at Barnhill. Sunlight and fresh air were regarded as beneficial, and patients were wheeled out in their beds onto the balconies seen here in front of the wards to soak up the elements. Under the NHS the sanatorium was renamed Barnhill Hospital, but soon became superfluous to requirements and was closed in 1958.

A handwritten note on the back of this picture describes it as 'Perth Pipe Band, Saturday 23rd May 1914, at the Sanatorium'. It was common for bands to provide entertainment at such institutions, often as part of special fund-raising events.

Kinnoull Hill provides a dramatic and distinctive backdrop to the east of the city. It has always been popular with Perth people, who have enjoyed the walk to its summit to take in the views either alone or in company. This would have been well understood by a local man like Lord Dewar when he presented the hill to the city in 1923. It was also a meeting place for young lovers, but in 1580 the Kirk forbade courting couples from visiting a cave known as the Dragon's Hole on the rocky face of the hill. Anyone found flouting the Kirk's directive would have to pay a fine of £1 Scots to the poor. The cave got its name because of an ancient belief that it was once the lair of a fearsome beast. William Wallace was also thought to have used it as a hideout, but neither he nor the dragon is actually known to have occupied it.

'The Summit of Delight on the Top of Kinnoull Hill, Perth.'